All About Beetles
by The Bug Collective
AF485974

Table of Content

INTRODUCTION

Introduction to Beetles

Imagine a world filled with a breathtaking array of colors, shapes, and sizes. A world where tiny creatures roam the earth, exhibiting remarkable adaptations and playing vital roles within their ecosystems. Welcome to the intriguing world of beetles.

Beetles, scientifically known as Coleoptera, are a diverse group of insects that encompass nearly 400,000 described species, making them the most diverse and successful group of animals on the planet. From intricately patterned ladybugs to impressively armored stag beetles, these fascinating creatures can be found in nearly every corner of the Earth, from the tallest mountains to the depths of our oceans.

In this chapter, we will embark on a journey to discover the enchanting world of beetles. Whether you are a curious nature enthusiast or a young explorer, we promise to make this journey exciting, educational, and even a little fun!

Unlike other insects, beetles possess a hardened outer covering called the exoskeleton, which serves as their armor against the world. This exoskeleton is comprised of a series of plates called elytra, which protect the delicate wings folded beneath them. It's almost like they wear their own little superhero costumes!

Now, let's meet some of the hilarious and extraordinary beetles that inhabit our planet. First, we have the Bombardier beetle. This clever little insect has a unique defense mechanism. When threatened, it can shoot a boiling hot, noxious chemical spray out of its rear end! Talk about having a fiery temper, right?

Next up, we have the clown beetle, aptly named for its vibrant and clown-like appearance. With its colorful spots and amusing antics, this beetle is surely the life of the insect party. You just can't help but smile when you see its jolly face.

But the funniest of them all has to be the dung beetle. Yes, you heard that correctly! These industrious insects spend their days rolling around balls of animal dung, which they use as a source of food and even as a home for their young. Talk about a stinky occupation!

Besides their humorous antics, beetles are also incredibly diverse in terms of size, shape, and behavior. From the minuscule feather-winged beetles to the mighty Hercules beetles with their formidable horns, each species has its own unique features that help it survive in its specific environment.

Beetles can be found in nearly every habitat imaginable. Some prefer the lush rainforests, while others thrive in sandy deserts or underwater environments. Their adaptability is truly astonishing. In fact, there are even beetles that have evolved to live solely in and around ant colonies, cunningly disguising themselves as ants to gain access to food and shelter. How's that for clever survival tactics?

But what makes beetles truly remarkable is their incredible impact on the world around us. Not only do they provide crucial services such as pollination and decomposition, but they also serve as indicators of environmental health. By studying beetles, scientists can gain valuable insights into the state of ecosystems and the effects of human activities on biodiversity.

Now, let's dive a little deeper into the extraordinary world of beetles. Did you know that some beetles have the ability to produce light? Yes, you heard that right! These magical glow-in-the-dark beetles, known as bioluminescent beetles, use their lightemitting organs called lanterns to communicate with each other. Imagine the sight of these beetles lighting up the night sky like tiny stars!

Beetles are also true architects in their own right. Take for instance the impressive leaf-cutter ants that sculpt and shape entire fragments of leaves, creating elaborate nests to house their colonies. These ants may be small, but their collective effort can result in intricate and highly organized structures that even human architects would envy.

Speaking of architects, the bombardier beetle, which we mentioned earlier, is not only famous for its defense mechanism but also for its ingenious burrowing prowess. This beetle can dig intricate tunnels underground, creating a cozy and safe haven for itself. It carefully constructs its home with precise design, ensuring stability and protection against predators.

But beetles' architectural talents don't stop there. Have you ever heard of the jewel beetle? These magnificent insects, adorned with vibrant and metallic-colored exoskeletons, are known for their incredible flying abilities. They gracefully maneuver through the air with such precision and grace that their flight patterns resemble a beautifully choreographed dance.

In addition to their extraordinary abilities, beetles play a vital role in nature's cycles. Many species are important pollinators, ensuring the reproduction of plants and the production of fruits and seeds.

Without beetles, our world would be a dull and food-scarce place.

Now, it's time to put on your explorer's hat and venture into the world of beetles. Remember, these incredible creatures not only bring wonder and amazement but also teach us valuable lessons about resilience, adaptation, and the delicate balance of nature.

So, whether you are captivated by the magic of the natural world, intrigued by the intricate designs of these tiny architects, or simply looking for an adventure within the pages of a book, join us as we unravel the mysteries and wonders of the enchanting world of beetles.

Get ready to be amazed, inspired, and maybe even a little bit creeped out by the incredible diversity and beauty that the world of beetles has to offer. Step into their world, and prepare to see nature through a whole new set of eyes. Welcome to the extraordinary world of beetles, where astonishment awaits at every turn.

Turn the page, and let the journey begin!

CHAPTER 1

The World of Beetles

Beetles are an incredibly diverse and fascinating group of insects, inhabiting almost every corner of the world. From tropical rainforests and deserts to your own backyard, beetles can be found in a wide range of habitats. In this chapter, we will explore the incredible diversity and adaptability of these remarkable creatures.

Beetles can be found in nearly every habitat on Earth, including forests, grasslands, wetlands, and even freshwater ecosystems. With over 400,000 known species and countless more yet to be discovered, they are the largest group of insects and also one of the most successful.

One of the reasons for their success is their incredible adaptability. Beetles have evolved to fill countless ecological niches, each with its own unique set of challenges. Some beetles have specialized mouthparts for feeding on specific types of plants, while others have developed strong jaws for capturing prey.

The world of beetles is filled with an incredible array of shapes, sizes, and colors. From tiny beetles that are barely visible to the naked eye to large and impressive species like the Goliath beetle, which can reach lengths of up to 4.5 inches, beetles come in all shapes and sizes. Their colors can range from dull browns and blacks to vibrant greens, blues, and reds, often serving as a form of camouflage or warning to potential predators.

Beyond their appearances, beetles possess amazing abilities that children might find funny and entertaining. Did you know that some beetles, like the whistling beetles, can create music?

These unique beetles produce sounds by rubbing or vibrating specific body parts together. Imagine a beetle orchestra with each beetle playing a different instrument, creating a symphony of amusing sounds and melodies!

Furthermore, there are beetles with extraordinary defense mechanisms. Take, for example, the bombardier beetle. When threatened, it can release a burst of hot, foul-smelling chemicals from its abdomen. This spray can reach temperatures of up to 212 degrees Fahrenheit! Kids can imagine this peculiar beetle as a little firebreathing dragon, ready to defend itself against any danger with a comical, smelly surprise.

But not all beetles rely on offensive tactics for defense. Some have developed a fantastic disguise to hide from predators. The tortoise beetles, for instance, have flattened bodies with extensions that resemble thorns or spines, making them look like tiny armored tanks. Kids can envision these beetles participating in a humorous parade, impersonating miniature soldiers with their amusing tank-like appearances.

Another fascinating aspect of beetles is their incredible variety of behaviors. Some beetles are highly social, living in large colonies and working together to build complex nests. Others are solitary hunters, relying on stealth and agility to catch their prey. There are even beetles that have developed incredible adaptations, such as the bolas spider-hunting beetle. This witty beetle uses a sticky string attached to its antennae to mimic the movements of a spider's prey, tricking the spider into becoming its meal instead. This clever trickster beetle can be imagined as a mischievous comedian playing pranks on its unsuspecting spider friends.

Now, let's dive deeper into the intriguing world of beetles and explore some additional fascinating aspects:

Did you know that some beetles have such unusual shapes that they look like comical characters straight out of a cartoon? Take, for instance, the weevil beetles with their long, curved snouts. These snouts are not only useful for feeding on plants but also give them a funny appearance, almost as if they were wearing a peculiar hat! Kids can have a good laugh imagining these beetles with their unique hairstyles and how they might use their snouts for playful adventures.

Moving on, there are beetles with peculiar dietary habits that might tickle children's sense of humor. For example, the dung beetle, as the name suggests, relies on animal droppings as its primary source of food. These resourceful beetles often roll balls of dung and push them around to use as a food source or for breeding purposes. While this may sound odd to us, it is a fascinating and important behavior in the world of beetles. Kids can giggle at the thought of beetles dancing around with their dung balls, imagining them as comical little comedians rolling their props on a grand stage.

The world of beetles is not only a place of scientific wonder but also a source of endless entertainment and inspiration. From the hilarious features to their extraordinary abilities, beetles have captured the hearts and imagination of people of all ages. So, let's continue our exploration of the beetle kingdom and uncover even more incredible facts and curious anecdotes that will bring laughter and amazement to both young and old

CHAPTER 2

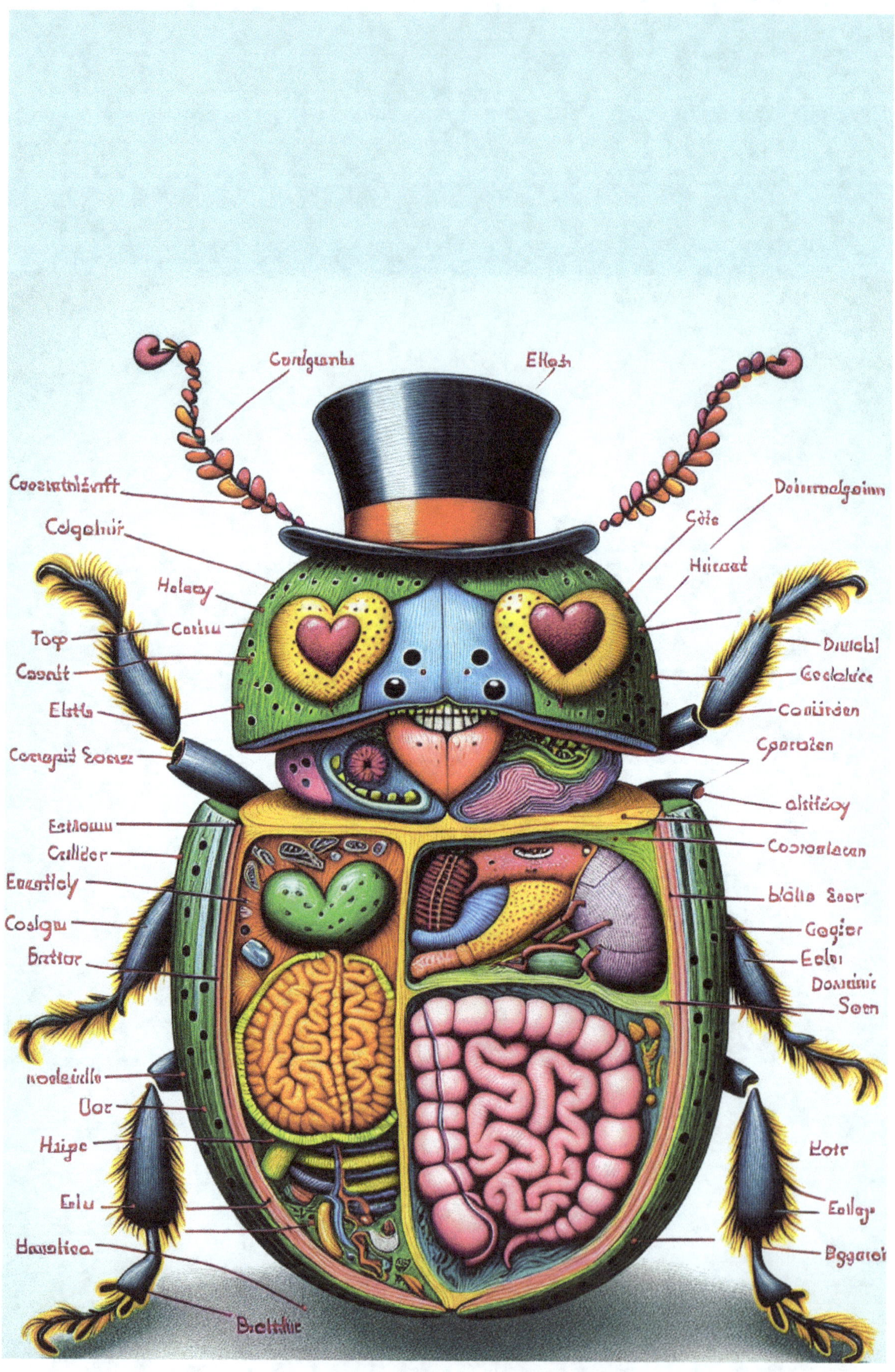
Cartigantu
Ekoh
Doumalgainn
Còte
Hiraet
Cosrattlevft
Cdgohir
Holeay
Carlu
Top
Casalt
Eltta
Corapid Sonz
Druhhl
Ecolchee
Conitéen
Cpeeaten
altiéoy
Cosroslacan
Estlomu
Callder
Enuctloy
Coslgu
Batlor
blalla Sour
Gogier
Eclu
Dominic
Seen
noeteidllo
Uor
Haipc
Elu
Hauslica
Hotr
Eollgo
Bggetoi
Bieltlue

Anatomy of an Ant

Beetles, those tiny wonders of the insect world, have always had a special place in our hearts. With their fascinating features and unique characteristics, they capture our imagination and spark our curiosity. In this chapter, we will take a closer look at the intricate anatomy of a beetle, diving deep into the amazing structures that make up these extraordinary creatures.

1. Head:

The beetle's head, like a little command center, is located at the front of its body. It is home to many important and peculiar features. Let's start with those big compound eyes! These remarkable eyes are a beetle's superpower, allowing them to see in multiple directions all at once. It's like having eyes at the back of their heads, only without the awkward head-turning. Some beetle species even have different types of eyes, like pinhead-sized eyespots on their antennae to keep an eye out for danger. Talk about being "all eyes"! But that's not all! Beetles are also blessed with a pair of flexible antennae, which act like their sensory superhero tools. These antennae help beetles detect smells, vibrations, and even taste their environment. It's like having an invisible sniffing and tasting superpower! Just imagine a beetle walking down the street, sniffing the air and tasting every delicious scent along the way. They could be the ultimate food critics or scent detectives!

2. Thorax:

Moving on to the middle section of a beetle's body, we find the mighty thorax. This crucial segment houses a beetle's vital organs and muscles that keep them going. You see, beetles are champions when it comes to moving their six legs. Their thorax is like a gym, packed with powerful muscles that allow them to perform impressive feats of strength. Some beetles can lift objects many times heavier than themselves, like tiny Hercules' bench-pressing enormous weights. Maybe they have their own tiny beetle gyms, complete with minuscule dumbbells and exercise equipment!

Apart from being a muscle powerhouse, the thorax acts as a protective armor for the beetle's internal organs. It's like a beetle's own superhero shield, safeguarding everything on the inside from unexpected bumps and scrapes. Just imagine if we had an invisible shield wrapped around our chest, protecting our hearts and lungs while we go about our daily adventures. Beetles truly have a fantastic defense mechanism!

3. Abdomen:

Now, let's journey to the rear section of a beetle's body, where we find the abdomen. Although the abdomen may not seem as exciting as the other parts, it plays an essential role in a beetle's survival. This segmented section houses many important systems, including the digestive, reproductive, and respiratory systems. Just like us, beetles need food, reproduce to continue their lineage, and breathe to stay alive. Talk about living the beetle life!

But here's a remarkable fact. Some beetles have developed specialized organs within their abdomen, which produce magnificent chemical potions. These magical concoctions can serve as defense mechanisms, deterring potential attackers with noxious smells or toxic secretions. It's like having a hidden perfume factory or an invisible shield, ensuring beetles stay safe and protected. They are the ultimate chemical wizards of the insect world!

4. Elytra:

Ah, the elytra, those elegant capes that turn beetles into the fashionistas of the insect realm. Elytra are the hardened forewings that cover and protect the delicate hindwings underneath, like fashionable coats for every occasion. But here's the twist: not all elytra are created equal! Some beetles have evolved specialized elytra for particular purposes. For example, the bombardier beetle possesses elytra paired with a fascinating defense mechanism. When threatened, it can shoot a hot, toxic chemical at its enemies, defending itself like a miniature fire-breathing dragon! Imagine having a dazzling cape that can shoot flames. That would undoubtedly make life more exciting!

But if defense isn't their game, some beetles take on an entirely different approach. They have elytra that resemble flowers, imitating the appearance of colorful petals. Why, you ask? Well, some beetles are sneaky and cunning. They use this clever costume party trick to either allure unsuspecting pollinators, like bees or butterflies, or to discourage predators from thinking they're tasty treats. It's like playing hide-and-seek while dressed as a beautiful bouquet. Such clever little tricksters!

5. Exoskeleton:

Lastly, we come to the armor-clad hero of every beetle's body: the exoskeleton. Imagine wearing sturdy, protective armor throughout your entire life—that's the beetle's reality. Their exoskeletons provide remarkable support and safeguard their vulnerable insides from harm. It's like having an invisible suit of armor that never needs polishing!

But the exoskeleton is not just for show. Beetles have an incredible ability to conserve water, and their exoskeletons play a crucial role in this seemingly magical feat. You see, beetles don't have lungs like we do. Instead, they have a tracheal system that allows oxygen to reach their tissues. The exoskeleton's toughness helps to prevent excessive water loss through evaporation, aiding beetles in their quest for survival. So not only are beetles amazingly armored adventurers, but they are also clever superheroes adapting to their environment in astonishing ways. Talk about being fantastic superheroes!

Understanding the detailed anatomy of a beetle transports us into the marvelous world of these small yet remarkable creatures. Whether you're a young reader fascinated by their miniature superpowers or an adult marveling at their evolutionary feats, exploring the intricate workings of beetles is a captivating journey. So let's put on our invisible microscope and embark on this thrilling adventure into the inner world of beetles!

CHAPTER 3

Б
П
З
2
3
4

The Life Cycle of a Beetle

Beetles, like many other insects, go through a fascinating and complex life cycle that consists of four distinct stages: egg, larva, pupa, and adult. Each stage plays a crucial role in the development and survival of these remarkable creatures. Let's delve deeper into the intricacies of the beetle's life cycle and explore the remarkable adaptations that allow them to thrive in diverse ecosystems.

1. Egg Stage:

The life cycle of a beetle begins with the egg stage. The female beetle carefully selects a suitable location to lay her eggs, ensuring they are placed where the larvae will find adequate food upon hatching. Beetles have evolved different egglaying strategies, and their eggs vary in size, shape, color, and placement. Some beetles lay their eggs individually, attaching them to leaves or bark, while others form clusters, attaching them to a substrate or hiding them in soil.

The eggs of beetles exhibit remarkable diversity in appearance. They can be round, oval, cylindrical, or even flattened, providing camouflage and protection from predators or parasitic insects during this vulnerable stage. These variations in egg morphology are often adaptive, ensuring they blend into their respective habitats. Some beetles lay eggs with a sticky gel-like substance, helping them adhere to particular surfaces or even underwater.

Eggs also have varying durations of dormancy, ensuring that the larvae hatch when environmental conditions are suitable. In some species, embryos can remain in a state of suspended development for extended periods, hatching only when triggered by specific environmental cues, such as temperature, moisture, or the presence of certain chemicals.

2. Larval Stage:

Once the eggs hatch, the larvae, commonly known as grubs, emerge. The larval stage is a time of intense growth and development. Beetles display an astonishing diversity of larval morphologies and feeding habits, adapting to the resource availability and ecological niches they occupy.

Some larvae have distinct body shapes, with segmented bodies and welldeveloped legs, allowing them to navigate through different microhabitats and substrates. Others appear grub-like, lacking prominent legs, but instead, they possess strong mandibles for feeding. The mandibles may be adapted for chewing plant material, capturing prey, or breaking down decaying organic matter. These adaptations ensure the larvae acquire the necessary nutrients for growth.

The diet of beetle larvae varies greatly among species. While some larvae are herbivorous and feed on plant matter, others are carnivorous, preying on small invertebrates or scavenging organic matter. Certain beetle larvae, such as the highly specialized dung beetles, exclusively consume dung as their primary food source. This diversity of diets is a testament to the vast array of ecological roles beetles play in ecosystems worldwide.

Beetle larvae undergo multiple molts as they grow, shedding their increasing size. The intervals between molts are crucial for the larvae to rest, heal, and allocate energy resources for further development. The final molt usually indicates readiness for the next stage of the life cycle, the pupa stage.

3. Pupa Stage:

After the larval stage, beetles enter the pupal stage, characterized by the formation of a protective casing called a pupa. Inside this casing, the larvae undergo a remarkable transformation through the process of metamorphosis. This stage is a time of rest and internal reorganization as the structures of the larva break down and reassemble into the adult form.

During pupation, dramatic changes occur within the pupal case. The beetle's body tissues break down into a liquid-like substance, undergoing cellular reorganization to form the adult body structures. This process includes the development of wings, the reformation of complex internal systems, and the growth of external features such as legs, antennae, and specialized mouthparts.

The duration of the pupal stage varies across beetle species and can last from a few days to several months. The external appearance of pupae also varies greatly. Some beetle pupae are enclosed in sturdy, protective cases constructed from fecal matter, wood debris, or soil particles. Others are bare and rely on their hidden location for protection. Certain pupae are even equipped with sharp spines or bristles, acting as deterrents against potential predators.

4. Adult Stage:

Upon completing the pupal stage, the fully developed adult beetle emerges from the pupal case. The freshly emerged beetle may initially have soft, pale-colored exoskeletons, but these gradually harden and darken within a few hours, allowing the beetle to take on its typical adult appearance.

The adult stage is the culmination of the beetle's life cycle and the time when reproduction, feeding, and other adult behaviors take place. The adult beetles are equipped with all the necessary adaptations for survival in their respective habitats.

Beetles have long been known for their extraordinary diversity, encompassing hundreds of thousands of species worldwide. Their wings enable flight, allowing them to disperse, find mates, and locate suitable food sources. The structure of their mouthparts determines their feeding behavior, which can range from chewing vegetation to piercing and sucking fluids from fruits, flowers, or even the bodies of other insects.

The longevity of the adult stage varies significantly among beetle species. Some adult beetles live for only a few weeks, while others can survive for several years, using their extended lifespan to contribute to ecosystem processes, participate in pollination, or engage in interactions with other organisms.

Understanding the life cycle of a beetle provides valuable insights into their ecology, behavior, and overall biology. It highlights the intricate strategies and adaptations that beetles have developed to thrive in diverse environments. From tiny eggs to powerful adults, beetles continue to captivate scientists and nature enthusiasts worldwide with their remarkable life cycle and their essential role in ecosystems.

CHAPTER 4

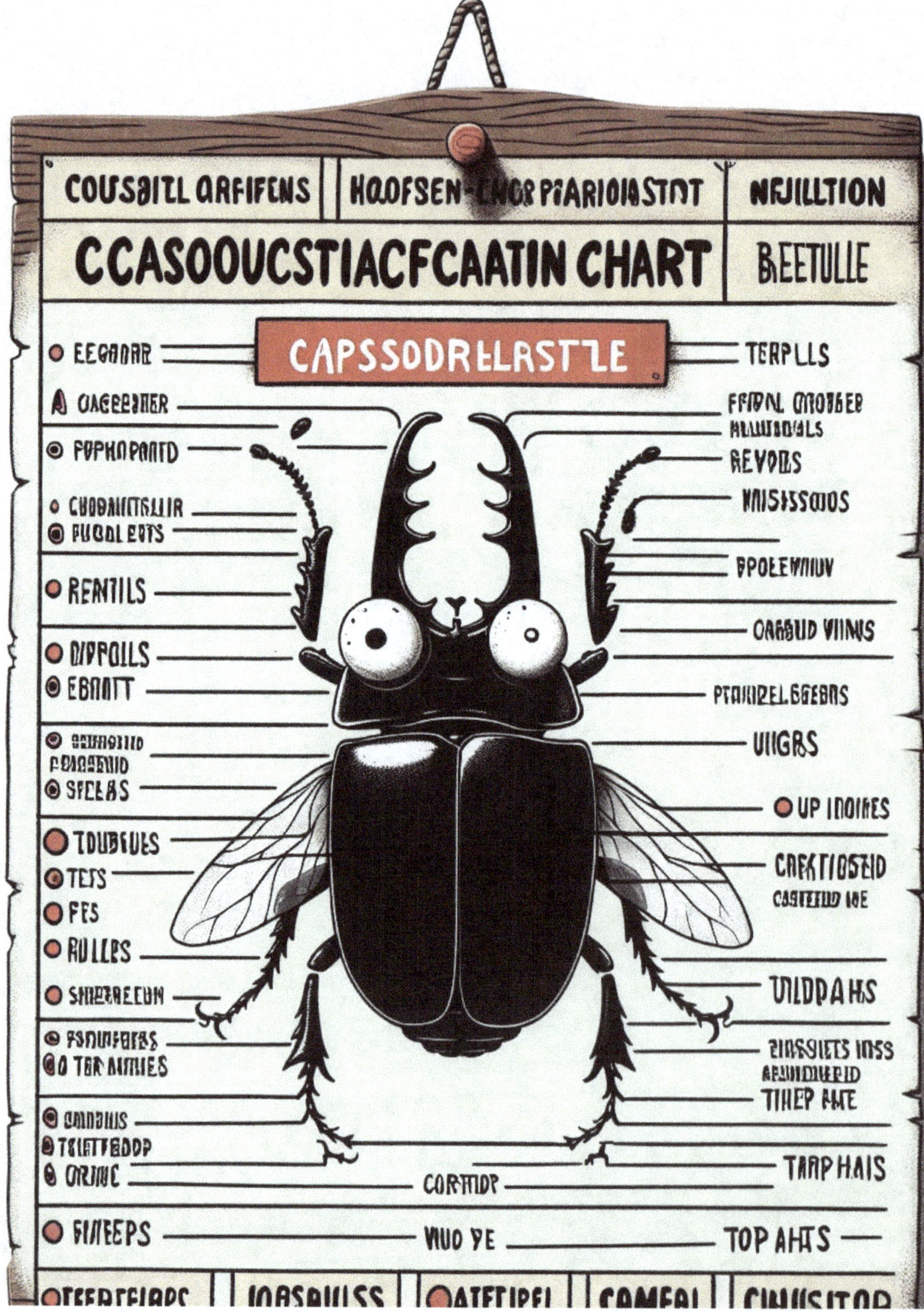
CLASSIFICATION CHART
CAPSODRELASTLE
BEETLE

Classification of a Beetle

Classification is an essential aspect of understanding the vast diversity of beetles. With over 400,000 known species, beetles make up the largest order of insects, known as Coleoptera. This chapter delves into the fascinating world of beetle classification, exploring the different levels of taxonomy and the characteristics used to categorize these incredible creatures.

At the highest level, beetles belong to the animal kingdom, known as Animalia. This kingdom encompasses a wide range of organisms, including humans, animals, insects, and other living creatures. Beetles, being part of this diverse kingdom, exhibit characteristics common to animals, such as being multicellular, eukaryotic organisms.

Moving further down the classification hierarchy, beetles are classified under the phylum Arthropoda, which includes insects, arachnids, crustaceans, and other jointed-legged creatures. Arthropods, characterized by segmented bodies, rigid exoskeletons, and paired jointed appendages, are incredibly diverse and comprise the largest number of species within the animal kingdom.

Within the arthropods, beetles fall into the class Insecta, along with other insects like butterflies, bees, flies, and mosquitoes. Insects are distinguished by their threepart body structure, consisting of a head, thorax, and abdomen, as well as having three pairs of legs and usually two pairs of wings. This class is exceptionally diverse, with insects occupying almost every imaginable habitat on Earth.

Beetles, specifically, are then categorized into the order Coleoptera, derived from the Greek words "koleos," meaning sheath, and "pteron," meaning wing. This name refers to the unique feature of beetles, possessing hardened forewings called elytra that protect and cover the delicate hind wings used for flight. The elytra, often adorned with various colors and patterns, serve as a protective shield against predators and environmental hazards.

Within the order Coleoptera, beetles are further divided into a multitude of families. Some common families include Carabidae (ground beetles), Scarabaeidae (scarab beetles), Curculionidae (weevils), Cerambycidae (longhorn beetles), Buprestidae (metallic wood-boring beetles), and Staphylinidae (rove beetles). Each family has its distinct set of characteristics that differentiate the beetles within, such as body shape, mouthpart structure, habitat preferences, and feeding habits.

To ensure correct identification, scientists look closely at various aspects of a beetle's morphology. These include attributes such as size, shape, coloration, antennae length, mouthpart structure, leg structure, the presence or absence of specific features like horns or spines, and even microscopic details of the exoskeleton. Additionally, genetic analysis plays a crucial role in confirming the classification of beetles and resolving complex taxonomic relationships.

The process of classifying beetles involves taxonomists who analyze and compare specimens, consult scientific literature, and meticulously examine the beetles' physical traits. These traits are then used to group beetles into species, genera, families, and so on, based on shared characteristics and evolutionary relationships. However, it's important to note that due to the vastness of beetle diversity, misclassification and reclassification are not uncommon as new information is discovered and our knowledge deepens.

While the number of identified beetle species is impressive, researchers believe that many more species are yet to be discovered, particularly in remote or unexplored regions of the world. Scientists and collectors frequently embark on expeditions to gather specimens and expand our understanding of beetle diversity. Furthermore, advancements in technology, such as DNA sequencing, allow for more accurate identification and classification of beetles, helping to uncover new species and clarify previously uncertain relationships.

Classification not only helps scientists organize and understand the vast beetle diversity but also offers insights into their evolutionary relationships. By comparing similarities and differences between beetle species, researchers can unravel the evolutionary patterns that have shaped these remarkable creatures over millions of years. Classification also aids in ecological studies, conservation efforts, and understanding the role beetles play in ecosystems worldwide.

Let's take a closer look at some of the families within the order Coleoptera:

1. Carabidae (Ground Beetles): This family is known for its diverse and predatory beetles. Ground beetles have elongated bodies, powerful mandibles, and are often found in habitats such as forests, grasslands, or near bodies of water. They play a vital role in controlling populations of pests and are considered beneficial insects in agricultural ecosystems.

2. Scarabaeidae (Scarab Beetles): Scarabs are perhaps the most well-known beetle family, including famous members like dung beetles and sacred scarabs. They are characterized by their stout bodies, clubbed antennae, and unique behaviors, such as rolling dung balls and burying them as a food source or breeding habitat. Scarabs have significant ecological importance, as they aid in nutrient cycling and soil health.

3. Curculionidae (Weevils): Weevils are easily recognizable by their elongated snouts or rostrums, which they use for feeding and oviposition. This family is incredibly diverse, with weevils inhabiting various habitats, including forests, grasslands, and cultivated crops. Weevils are notorious agricultural pests, causing damage to crops such as grains, fruits, and vegetables.

4. Cerambycidae (Longhorn Beetles): Longhorn beetles derive their name from their characteristic long antennae, often exceeding the length of their bodies. They come in a wide array of shapes, sizes, and colors, with some species possessing vibrant patterns or mimicry to deter predators. While most longhorn beetles are harmless, some species can be damaging to timber and may require pest control measures.

5. Buprestidae (Metallic Wood-Boring Beetles): This family includes some of the most visually striking beetles, known for their shining metallic colors, such as emerald, copper, or gold. Metallic wood-boring beetles inhabit forests and woodlands, often infesting and damaging trees. They play a vital role in decomposing deadwood, aiding in nutrient recycling and contributing to forest ecosystem dynamics.

6. Staphylinidae (Rove Beetles): Rove beetles have elongated bodies and short elytra, making them resemble ants at first glance. This family is highly diverse and can be found in a multitude of habitats, including leaf litter, decaying matter, and soil. Rove beetles are known for their predator-prey interactions and are important contributors to decomposer communities.

Beyond the families mentioned above, there are numerous other families within the order Coleoptera, each with its own unique characteristics and adaptations. Some examples include Elateridae (click beetles), Lampyridae (fireflies), Coccinellidae (ladybugs), and Chrysomelidae (leaf beetles). These families showcase the incredible diversity of beetles, with adaptations for various lifestyles, feeding habits, and habitats.

For instance, click beetles (Elateridae) are known for their ability to snap their bodies into the air when they are on their backs. This click mechanism allows them to flip themselves over and escape from predators or difficult situations. Fireflies (Lampyridae) are famous for their bioluminescence, producing light through a complex chemical reaction. This light is used for mate attraction and communication. Ladybugs (Coccinellidae) are beloved for their colorful spotted appearance and their voracious appetite for aphids and other soft-bodied insects, making them valuable natural pest controllers. Leaf beetles (Chrysomelidae) are often found on plants, feeding on leaves and sometimes causing damage to crops or ornamental plants.

While beetles are incredibly diverse, they do share some common characteristics that set them apart from other insects. One of the key features is the presence of elytra, the hardened forewings that protect the delicate hind wings. The elytra form the characteristic shell-like covering over the body and are usually multi-colored or patterned, providing camouflage or warning signals. Another shared trait is the presence of biting mouthparts, used for feeding on a wide range of food sources, including plant material, other insects, fungi, and even carrion.

Beetles also exhibit a remarkable array of adaptations to various habitats and ecological niches. Some beetles have evolved to be excellent burrowers, with shovel-like heads and robust forelegs for digging tunnels in the soil. Others have specialized mouthparts for piercing and sucking, enabling them to feed on plant sap or the blood of vertebrate hosts. Beetles that live in aquatic environments have often evolved streamlined bodies, flattened legs for swimming, and modified respiratory systems to extract oxygen from the water.

As new technologies and research methods continue to advance, the classification of beetles will undoubtedly evolve. With the ongoing exploration of remote and unexplored regions, along with the discovery of new species, our understanding of beetle diversity and their classification will expand. This, in turn, will deepen our appreciation for these incredible creatures and their importance in ecosystems worldwide.

The classification of beetles is a dynamic and ever-evolving field of study. From the highest level of the animal kingdom to the specific families within the order Coleoptera, classification provides a framework for understanding the vast diversity of beetles. By examining physical traits, studying genetic relationships, and exploring their ecological roles, scientists can unravel the mysteries of these fascinating creatures and shed light on their evolutionary history.

CHAPTER 5

Beetle Habitats

Beetles, being one of the most diverse groups of insects, can be found in a wide variety of habitats across the globe. These incredible creatures have adapted to live in almost every environment imaginable, from lush rainforests to arid deserts, and from freshwater ecosystems to the depths of caves. This chapter delves into some of the fascinating habitats where beetles thrive.

1. Forests:

Beetles are abundant in forest ecosystems, which cover about 30% of the Earth's land surface. They can be found in both deciduous and coniferous forests, feeding on plant matter, dead wood, and even other insects. Forest beetle communities are incredibly diverse, with various species occupying different niches. Some species prefer the forest floor, feeding on leaf litter or burrowing into the soil, while others dwell within the canopy or on the bark of trees. These beetles play essential roles in nutrient cycling, decomposition, and as food sources for other organisms.

In deciduous forests, beetles such as the stag beetles (Lucanidae) are commonly found. These impressive beetles have long and branching mandibles that they use to compete for mates or defend their territories. In coniferous forests, we find species such as the bark beetles (Scolytinae), which dig galleries under the tree bark, affecting the health and stability of the trees. The relationships between beetles and trees are complex and can have significant ecological consequences.

2. Grasslands:

Beetles have also adapted to live in grasslands and prairies, which are characterized by vast stretches of open land with an abundance of grasses and flowering plants. These open habitats provide a rich food source for herbivorous beetles. Some species specialize in feeding on specific plants, while others are generalists that consume a variety of plant material. Additionally, many beetles in grasslands are specialized in feeding on decaying organic matter, playing crucial roles in nutrient cycling, decomposition, and soil enrichment.

Grasslands support a wide variety of beetles, including scarab beetles (Scarabaeidae), which are prominent herbivores feeding on grasses and contribute to nutrient recycling through their dung-rolling behaviors. Other grassland beetles, such as ground beetles (Carabidae), are important predators that help control population levels of insects, including agricultural pests. The diversity and abundance of beetles in grasslands make these habitats vital to many ecosystems.

3. Wetlands:

Wetlands, including marshes, swamps, and bogs, are home to a diverse range of beetles. These water-rich ecosystems provide ample food sources, such as algae, aquatic plants, and decomposing organic matter. Some beetles have even evolved specific adaptations to thrive in aquatic habitats, such as modified legs for swimming or breathing tubes to extract oxygen from water. Additionally, wetland beetles contribute to the ecosystem by serving as pollinators or as prey for other organisms.

Water beetles (Dytiscidae), for instance, are skilled swimmers and divers, with streamlined bodies and paddle-like legs enabling them to pursue their prey underwater. These beetles have air stores beneath their wings, which they replenish by returning to the water surface periodically. They play crucial roles in wetland ecosystems by consuming insect larvae and tadpoles, while also serving as food for birds and fish.

4. Deserts:

Despite the extreme conditions, beetles have successfully colonized desert habitats worldwide. These resilient insects have evolved various mechanisms to conserve water and tolerate temperature fluctuations. Some desert beetles are even adept at collecting moisture from fog or condensation, enabling them to survive in arid regions. These beetles often have specialized behaviors and adaptations to avoid excessive water loss, such as burrowing during the day and being active at night when temperatures are cooler. In desert ecosystems, beetles play valuable roles in decomposition, nutrient cycling, and as a crucial food source for other desertdwelling organisms. ### beetles (Cicindelinae), known for their incredible speed and predatory abilities, are often found in sandy desert habitats. They have long, slender legs and large, powerful jaws, which allow them to ambush prey or chase down insects across the scorching desert sands. These remarkable beetles are well-adapted to the arid conditions and demonstrate the tenacity and resourcefulness of desertdwelling insects.

5. Caves:

The mysterious realm of caves is also home to a unique array of beetle species. These underground habitats offer a stable environment with constant temperatures and high humidity, making them suitable for beetles adapted to dark and moist conditions. Many cave-dwelling beetles have lost their wings as they no longer need them in the lightless underground world. Some species have evolved specialized adaptations, such as elongated appendages or sensory structures, to navigate and locate resources in the darkness. Additionally, cave beetles often have unique interactions with other cave-dwelling organisms, such as bats or cave crustaceans.

6. Mountains:

Beetles can be found at high elevations, including mountains and alpine regions. These habitats pose challenges such as low temperatures and limited food availability, but many beetle species have adapted to these conditions. Some beetles have developed specialized adaptations, such as thickened exoskeletons or the ability to tolerate freezing temperatures. Mountain beetles often have short life cycles to take advantage of the brief periods of warm weather during the summer. These resilient insects contribute to the ecosystem by pollinating alpine flowers, decomposing organic matter, and serving as a food source for alpine birds and mammals.

One example of a mountain-dwelling beetle is the snow flea (Boreidae), which is not truly a flea but a small wingless insect. These tiny beetles are commonly found hopping on the surface of snowfields, scarfing down microscopic algae and fungi that flourish in the harsh alpine environments. They are a vital source of food for higher trophic levels and have developed unique adaptations to navigate icy surfaces.

7. Urban Environments:

Beetles are not confined solely to natural habitats; they have also adapted to urban environments. Urban parks, gardens, and even city streets can support a diversity of beetle species. Some beetles have become pests in urban areas, feeding on stored food products or landscaping plants, while others are beneficial predators of garden pests. Urban environments may provide new resources and shelter for beetles, allowing them to persist and even thrive amidst human activities. Studying beetles in urban settings can provide insights into their adaptability and ecological resilience.

The presence of beetles in cities highlights their remarkable ability to adapt to a wide range of conditions. Carabid beetles, commonly known as ground beetles, are often observed living among urban green spaces. These voracious predators contribute to pest control within the city, as they feedon insect larvae, slugs, and other small invertebrates. Additionally, various species of beetles can be found in gardens, where they play important roles as pollinators and decomposers. By studying beetles in urban environments, researchers can gain a better understanding of how these insects adapt to human-altered landscapes and potentially develop strategies for promoting their conservation.

Beetles have successfully colonized a wide range of habitats across the globe, showcasing their remarkable adaptability and diversity. From forests to grasslands, wetlands to deserts, and even caves and urban environments, beetles have found ways to thrive and contribute to ecosystem functioning. Understanding the unique adaptations and ecological roles of beetles in different habitats is crucial for their remarkable adaptability and diversity. From forests to grasslands, wetlands to deserts, and even caves and urban environments, beetles have found ways to thrive and contribute to ecosystem functioning. Understanding the unique adaptations and ecological roles of beetles in different habitats is crucial for their conservation and for maintaining the balance of our natural world.

CHAPTER 6

Beetle Behavior

Beetles are fascinating creatures with an intriguing array of behaviors. This chapter delves into the various aspects of their behavior, shedding light on their interactions with their environment and other organisms.

One prominent aspect of beetle behavior is their feeding habits. Beetles exhibit a diverse range of feeding strategies, depending on their species. Some beetles are herbivorous, feeding on plants and foliage. They have evolved specialized mouthparts to chew and consume plant material effectively. For instance, leaf beetles possess sharp, serrated mandibles that allow them to cut through tough plant tissues, while longhorn beetles use their elongated mouthparts to bore into wood and consume the cellulose within. Furthermore, some beetles have even formed symbiotic relationships with plants. For example, certain wood-boring beetles depend on fungi that break down wood fibers, enabling their digestion of this otherwise indigestible food source.

Others are carnivorous, preying on insects or even small vertebrates. These predatory beetles have sharp mandibles and are skilled hunters, employing tactics such as ambush or pursuit to capture their prey. They are well-adapted to their predatory lifestyle, possessing strong legs for tackling and restraining their prey, as well as robust jaws that enable them to deliver precise and powerful bites. Some tiger beetles are renowned for their incredible speed, using their well-developed mandibles to seize their prey. Additionally, some beetles have developed specialized adaptations to overcome the defenses of their prey. For example, ground beetles produce toxic chemicals that help immobilize their prey or deter potential predators.

Another fascinating behavior exhibited by beetles is their mating rituals. How beetles attract mates and reproduce varies greatly across species. Some beetles use visual cues, such as intricate body patterns or bright colors, to attract a mate. These visual displays often indicate the health and fitness of the individual, as well as their ability to provide resources during mating and reproduction. For instance, male fireflies emit flashes of light to attract females of the same species during their mesmerizing evening displays. Others rely on chemical signals, releasing pheromones into the air to communicate their availability and readiness for mating. These pheromones are species-specific and help beetles find suitable mates amidst a vast array of smells in their environment. For example, female longhorn beetles release pheromones that attract males from long distances, ensuring successful reproduction.

The courtship rituals of beetles can be elaborate and involve displays of strength, agility, or unique behaviors. For instance, some stag beetles engage in fierce battles with rival males, using their enlarged jaws to wrestle over territories and access to females, creating an impressive spectacle for onlookers. These rituals often serve to ensure successful mating and reproductive success by ensuring the strongest and most genetically compatible individuals mate. Additionally, some male beetles have evolved manipulative behaviors to ensure successful mating, such as providing females with nuptial gifts like prey or plant materials. These gifts not only act as a demonstration of the male's ability to provide, but they can also influence the female's willingness to mate.

Beetles also engage in social behaviors, albeit to a lesser extent compared to other insects like ants or bees. Some species of beetles live in colonies or groups, where individuals work together to defend resources or care for their offspring. These social beetles communicate through various means, including touch, chemical signals, and vibrational cues. For example, burying beetles cooperate in burying small carcasses, creating an underground chamber where they lay their eggs and rear their larvae. The adults emit pheromones and engage in tactile communication to coordinate their efforts and ensure the survival of their offspring.

Social beetles can exhibit complex interactions and hierarchical structures within their colonies, showcasing their remarkable abilities to cooperate and coordinate with other individuals. For example, leafcutter ants employ division of labor, with some ants specializing in cutting and carrying leaves while others focus on tending the fungus gardens that provide their food. Similarly, dung beetles form social groups where individuals collaborate to locate and bury dung balls, ensuring a food source for themselves and their offspring. These cooperative behaviors allow beetles to share workloads, defend against predators, and optimize their chances of survival and reproductive success.

Additionally, beetles have developed remarkable mechanisms for defense and protection. Many species of beetles possess tough exoskeletons that provide physical protection against predators. The exoskeleton consists of a hard outer layer called the elytra, which protects the delicate wings and abdomen beneath. Some beetles have also evolved unique defense strategies, such as chemical warfare. These beetles can secrete noxious or toxic substances from specialized glands in their bodies, deterring potential predators. Ladybugs, for example, release a foul-tasting and smelly liquid when threatened, deterring predators from consuming them.

Furthermore, beetles display an impressive range of behaviors related to adaptation and survival. Some species burrow underground, creating elaborate tunnels and chambers for shelter and reproduction. Dung beetles, for instance, roll and bury dung balls underground, providing a safe environment for laying eggs and nourishment for their offspring. Other beetles have evolved the ability to roll into a protective ball when threatened, a behavior commonly referred to as "ballrolling." This behavior allows the beetles to shield themselves from harm, using their strong exoskeleton as a shield against potential predators.

In addition to their physical adaptations, beetles have also evolved intricate sensory systems that aid in their behavior and survival. They possess a wide range of sensory organs, including antennae, eyes, and sensory hairs spread across their bodies. These sensory organs enable them to detect and respond to various environmental cues. For example, beetles can detect pheromones released by potential mates or predators, allowing them to navigate and make informed decisions. Some beetles also have specialized structures on their antennae, known as sensilla, which help them sense vibrations in the air or substrate. These vibrations can provide crucial information about the presence of nearby organisms, potential threats, or suitable resources.

The behavior of beetles is further influenced by their physiological and ecological characteristics. Beetle species are adapted to different habitats, and their behavior reflects their ecological niche. For example, some beetles have evolved to live in aquatic environments. These aquatic beetles have adaptations such as hydrophobic exoskeletons that repel water, enabling them to move easily on the water's surface.

Some beetles even use bubbles of air captured beneath their wings as a temporary air supply while they navigate underwater. Similarly, desertdwelling beetles have behavioral adaptations to cope with arid conditions. They may be active during cooler times of the day or possess specialized anatomical structures that minimize water loss.

Moreover, beetle behavior can be influenced by external factors such as temperature, light, and seasonal changes. Some beetles exhibit diurnal behavior, being active during daylight hours, while others are nocturnal, thriving under cover of darkness. These diel patterns often relate to factors such as predator avoidance, resource availability, or temperature regulation. Additionally, behavioral changes may occur during different life stages. For instance, some beetles undergo complete metamorphosis, transitioning through egg, larval, pupal, and adult stages. The behaviors exhibited during each stage vary dramatically, allowing beetles to fulfill different ecological roles and adapt to changing environmental conditions.

Bottom line, he behavior of beetles is incredibly diverse and fascinating. Their feeding habits, mating rituals, social behaviors, defense mechanisms, and adaptations all contribute to their remarkable ability to survive and thrive in various environments. From herbivorous leaf beetles to predatory ground beetles, each species has evolved unique behaviors and strategies to ensure their survival and reproductive success. Understanding beetle behavior not only sheds light on their ecological roles but also provides insights into the complexity and diversity of the natural world.

CHAPTER 7

The Benefits of Beetles

Beetles, often overlooked and misunderstood creatures, play a vital role in our ecosystem and offer numerous benefits to the natural world. While some may view beetles as mere pests or nuisances, their contributions to the environment are truly remarkable. In this chapter, we will explore the various ways in which beetles benefit our planet and why we should appreciate these tiny, yet essential, creatures.

One significant benefit of beetles lies in their role as decomposers. Many beetles feed on decaying organic matter such as dead animals, plant material, and even dung. By consuming and breaking down these organic substances, beetles facilitate the recycling of nutrients back into the soil. This helps maintain soil fertility and promotes a healthy ecosystem. Without beetles, the accumulation of decaying matter would lead to an imbalance in nutrient cycles, disrupting the delicate web of life.

Interestingly, beetles have evolved various adaptations that allow them to efficiently decompose organic matter. For instance, burying beetles (Nicrophorus spp.) have specialized mouthparts and behaviors enabling them to bury small animal carcasses. By undertaking this burial process, the beetles not only consume the nutrients from the carcass but also prevent the spread of diseases and reduce competitor populations. This behavior showcases the intricate relationship between beetles and decomposition, further highlighting their importance in maintaining ecosystem balance.

Another essential contribution beetles make is in pollination. While bees may be the most renowned pollinators, beetles are surprisingly effective in this regard as well. Certain species of flower-visiting beetles, with their specialized mouthparts and structures, assist in the transfer of pollen from one flower to another. This process promotes plant reproduction, genetic diversity, and the production of fruits and seeds. In some regions, beetles are the primary pollinators, especially where bee populations have declined due to factors like habitat loss and pesticide use. Thus, beetles play a crucial role in maintaining the world's floral diversity.

It is fascinating to note that beetles have coevolved with flowering plants, resulting in remarkable adaptations for effective pollination. For example, certain orchid species have evolved flowers that resemble female beetles, attracting the male beetles that inadvertently pick up and transfer pollen in their attempts to mate with the flowers. This intricate dance between beetles and plants highlights the remarkable interconnectedness of species and their adaptations, underscoring the importance of conserving these relationships for the benefit of both beetles and plants.

Furthermore, some beetles serve as natural pest controllers. For instance, ladybird beetles (ladybugs) and ground beetles are voracious predators of harmful insects, including aphids, caterpillars, and beetles that damage crops. By preying on these pests, beetles help regulate their populations, reducing the need for harmful chemical pesticides in agriculture. This natural form of pest control not only benefits farmers by protecting their crops but also contributes to a more sustainable and environmentally friendly approach to farming.

The natural predator-prey relationships between beetles and pest insects are fascinating examples of nature's balance. For instance, ladybird beetles use chemical cues emitted by aphids to locate their prey efficiently. Some aquatic beetles even have specialized adaptations such as air bubbles held under their wings, enabling them to remain submerged while hunting for small invertebrates. These adaptations highlight the incredible diversity of beetles and their effectiveness in maintaining ecological equilibrium.

Beetles also play a vital role in nutrient cycling. Certain species, such as dung beetles, specialize in breaking down dung from mammalian herbivores. By burying and consuming dung, these beetles help speed up the decomposition process, prevent the spread of diseases, and recycle nutrients back into the soil. This process is particularly important in maintaining the balance of ecosystems where large herbivores exist, as it prevents the buildup of waste that can harm plant growth and contaminate water sources.

It is worth noting that dung beetles exhibit remarkable adaptations that enable them to efficiently utilize and decompose dung. For example, they have strong forelegs designed for digging and rolling dung balls, which they use both as a food source and as a site for breeding. Additionally, dung beetles navigate by using celestial cues such as the moon and the Milky Way, ensuring they efficiently bury their dung and establish suitable breeding grounds. These intricate behaviors and adaptations demonstrate the sophistication of dung beetles in nutrient cycling.

Another noteworthy contribution of beetles is their involvement in the process of primary and secondary succession. Primary succession occurs in places where there was no previous soil, such as after volcanic eruptions or glacier retreats. In these barren landscapes, beetles are often the first colonizers, arriving to feast on microscopic organisms and lichens that begin to grow in the early stages. Their feeding activities create organic material, which together with their waste, contributes to the eventual formation of soil that can support more complex life forms. The presence of beetles in these early stages of succession helps pave the way for the establishment of future plant communities and the overall regeneration of ecosystems.

In secondary succession, which occurs after a disturbance such as a fire or logging, beetles once again play a key role. They help break down dead plant material and release nutrients back into the soil, aiding in the recovery and regrowth of vegetation. Their presence promotes the expansion of plant species that are attracted to beetle-damaged wood, fostering a healthy and diverse forest ecosystem.

Additionally, some beetles specialize in feeding on fungal organisms that often inhabit dead plant material, effectively controlling fungal diseases and contributing to the resiliency of the regenerating ecosystem. Beyond their ecological contributions, beetles have also influenced human society throughout history. Some species, like the scarab beetles in ancient Egypt, held cultural and religious significance. The ancient Egyptians believed that these beetles symbolized resurrection and rebirth, often associating them with their sun god, Ra. Images of scarab beetles were commonly used as amulets and carved into jewelry, emphasizing the cultural importance of beetles in ancient societies.

Furthermore, beetles have even influenced human technology and innovation. Scientists have started studying beetle-inspired engineering, known as biomimicry, taking inspiration from the unique features of beetles to develop new technologies. For example, the structure of the ladybird beetle's wings has inspired the development of self-cleaning surfaces, as they possess special microstructures that repel dirt and water. Similarly, the bombardier beetle, with its ability to release a hot and noxious spray when threatened, has inspired the design of microfluidic devices that can deliver precise amounts of various substances. These examples highlight the incredible potential in harnessing the natural adaptations of beetles for human innovation and progress.

Beetles are far from insignificant creatures. They contribute immensely to the health and proper functioning of our ecosystems, from nutrient recycling and pollination to pest control and cultural significance. Recognizing and appreciating the many benefits that beetles offer can foster a greater understanding of the delicate balance of nature and encourage us to protect these incredible creatures for generations to come. The intricate adaptations, behaviors, and relationships that beetles possess further emphasize their significance and inspire further exploration into the depths of their wonderful world.

CHAPTER 8

Beetles and the Environment

Beetles play a crucial role in maintaining the balance of ecosystems and the health of our environment. Their impact extends far beyond their small size and inconspicuous appearance. In this chapter, we will delve deeper into the intricate ways in which beetles contribute to the environment and why their conservation is of utmost importance.

1. Ecosystem Services:

Beetles provide essential ecosystem services that benefit both plants and animals. One of their key roles is that of decomposers. Many species of beetles help break down decaying organic matter, such as fallen leaves, dead animals, and wood debris. By doing so, they facilitate the recycling of nutrients and the enrichment of soil quality, which is vital for the growth and survival of other organisms.

These decomposer beetles, often referred to as saprophages, play a significant role in nutrient cycling. They have unique adaptations that allow them to break down complex polymers found in organic matter, converting them into simpler forms. Some beetles possess specialized enzymes in their gut that aid in the digestion of tough plant materials, while others rely on a diverse community of microorganisms residing in their digestive systems to break down complex organic compounds. Through these processes, beetles release essential elements such as carbon, nitrogen, and phosphorus back into the ecosystem. Without beetles' efficient decomposition, the build-up of organic matter would lead to nutrient immobilization and hinder the growth of plants and other organisms.

In addition to decomposition, some beetles, such as burying beetles and dung beetles, play a crucial role in nutrient recycling by feeding on and dispersing animal waste. By burying dung, these beetles prevent the accumulation of harmful pathogens and reduce the risk of diseases for both wildlife and humans. Moreover, their activities enhance the fertility of the soil, promoting healthier vegetation growth.

2. Pollination:

Beetles are known as important pollinators, although they are often overshadowed by bees and butterflies. While feeding on nectar or pollen, beetles unintentionally transfer pollen between flowers, aiding in the reproduction of numerous flowering plants. Considering their long evolutionary history, beetles played a fundamental role in the early diversification of flowering plants, contributing to the wide array of colors, shapes, and sizes seen in their flowers.

Unlike bees and butterflies, beetles do not possess specialized mouthparts for efficient pollen transfer. Instead, they rely on their sheer numbers and the time they spend inside flowers. Some beetle species have fuzzy bodies that readily collect pollen, while others have mouthparts that allow them to scrape or chew on plants to access floral rewards. Due to their feeding habits, beetles are often attracted to large, bowl-shaped flowers with a strong scent or exposed reproductive parts that provide easy access to pollen and nectar.

While beetles are not as effective as bees in pollination, they play an essential role in specific ecosystems. They are particularly important in regions where bee populations are scarce or limited, such as high mountainous areas or colder regions. In such contexts, beetles become the primary pollinators, ensuring the reproduction of a variety of plant species.

3. Pest Control:

Interestingly, certain species of beetles are also valuable in pest control. Many beetles are voracious predators, feeding on various harmful insects and pests that can wreak havoc on crops and plants. This natural form of pest control helps maintain the balance of ecosystems and reduces the reliance on chemical pesticides that can have detrimental effects on the environment.

Ladybugs, for example, are well-known beetle predators that help control aphids, a common and destructive pest in gardens and agricultural fields. These beetles and others belonging to the Coccinellidae family are equipped with specialized mouthparts that allow them to pierce and consume soft-bodied insects like aphids. By preying on these pests, beetles act as natural biological control agents, reducing the need for harmful chemical pesticides.

Furthermore, beetles provide effective control against agricultural pests because they have developed various adaptations to locate and consume their prey. Some beetles use chemical cues emitted by insects in distress, while others employ visual or vibrational signals to detect potential prey. Their ability to detect pest populations and effectively control them makes beetles an important asset in sustainable agricultural practices.

4. Indicator Species:

Beetles can serve as indicators of environmental health and habitat quality. Some beetle species are highly sensitive to changes in their surroundings, such as pollution, deforestation, or alterations in climate patterns. Monitoring the presence and abundance of certain beetle species can provide valuable insights into the overall health of an ecosystem and help identify areas that require conservation efforts or further study. For instance, aquatic beetles are particularly sensitive to changes in water quality. The presence or absence of certain aquatic beetle species can indicate the level of pollutants in a water body. Additionally, the diversity and abundance of beetles in specific habitats can reflect the complexity and overall health of the ecosystem. Their sensitivity to disturbances makes beetles valuable biological indicators, aiding in environmental monitoring and conservation planning.

5. Threats to Beetles and Conservation Efforts:

Unfortunately, beetles, like many other insects, are facing numerous threats in today's rapidly changing world. Habitat destruction, pesticide use, climate change, and pollution are just a few of the significant challenges that beetles and their ecosystems face.

Habitat loss is one of the greatest threats to beetles. Urban expansion, intensive agricultural practices, and deforestation destroy their natural habitats, leaving them with limited space and resources to survive. Fragmentation and degradation of habitats also disrupt the natural interactions between beetles and their hosts or prey, leading to population declines and potential local extinctions.

Pesticide use, primarily in agriculture, poses substantial risks to beetles. Due to their wide range of feeding habits and behaviors, beetles may inadvertently come into contact with agricultural chemicals, leading to intoxication or death. The widespread use of neonicotinoids, a class of insecticides, has been particularly harmful to beetles, as they are highly toxic to many species. Climate change is another significant concern for beetles. Rising temperatures, altered precipitation patterns, and changing seasonal cycles can disrupt the delicate balance of beetle populations. Shifts in temperature and rainfall can affect beetle phenology, distribution, and overall abundance. Certain species may face difficulty in adapting to these changes, while others may be pushed beyond their climatic limits and face extinction.

To address these threats and protect beetle populations, conservation efforts focused on preserving their habitats and raising awareness about their ecological importance are crucial. Initiatives such as creating protected areas, implementing sustainable agricultural practices, and reducing pesticide use are essential steps towards ensuring the survival of these remarkable creatures.

Public education and engagement are also crucial for conservation success. By promoting positive attitudes towards beetles and their ecological roles, we can encourage individuals, communities, and policymakers to take action towards their conservation. Understanding the intrinsic value of beetles and their contributions to the environment is key to safeguarding the future of these remarkable creatures.

Beetles play vital roles in the environment, ranging from decomposition and pollination to pest control and acting as indicators of ecosystem health. Their preservation is critical for the well-being of our planet and its diverse ecosystems. By understanding and appreciating the significance of beetles in the environment, we can work together to protect and conserve these extraordinary creatures for futuregenerations to come. Here are some additional points to consider:

Invasive Species: Invasive species pose a significant threat to native beetle populations. When non-native beetles are introduced to new areas, they can outcompete and displace native species, disrupting the delicate ecological balance. These invasive beetles can have detrimental effects on ecosystems, such as damaging crops, trees, and other vegetation. Efforts to prevent the introduction and spread of invasive beetles are vital for protecting native biodiversity.

Important Food Source: Beetles also serve as an essential food source for many other animals. Insects, birds, reptiles, amphibians, and small mammals rely on beetles as a primary or supplemental food source. The decline or loss of beetle populations can have cascading effects on the entire food web, leading to disruptions in ecosystem functioning.

Bioindicators of Environmental Change: Due to their sensitivity to environmental changes, beetles can serve as bioindicators. By studying the presence, absence, or abundance of specific beetle species in different habitats, scientists can gather valuable information about the health and condition of ecosystems. Changes in beetle populations can indicate disturbances in habitat quality, climate change effects, or the impact of environmental management practices.

Conservation Strategies: Conservation efforts for beetles involve a range of approaches. Protecting and restoring natural habitats is essential to provide suitable conditions for beetle populations to thrive. This can include the creation of wildlife corridors, reforestation projects, and the preservation of wetlands and other critical habitats.

Reducing pesticide use and adopting more sustainable agricultural practices are also crucial for beetle conservation. Integrated pest management (IPM) techniques that minimize chemical pesticide use and focus on biological control methods can help maintain balanced ecosystems and protect beneficial beetle species.

Encouraging citizen science initiatives can also contribute to beetle conservation. Citizen scientists can help monitor beetle populations, collect data on species distributions, and contribute to important research and conservation efforts. By involving the community, individuals can play an active role in the conservation of beetles and their habitats.

CHAPTER 9

Beetles in Human History

Throughout history, beetles have played a significant role in human civilization. From symbols of power and protection to sources of inspiration for art and architecture, beetles have captivated the imagination of people across cultures and time periods.

One of the earliest recorded instances of beetles in human history can be traced back to ancient Egypt. The scarab beetle, known for its distinctive shape and association with the sun god Ra, held great religious and mythological significance in Egyptian society. Considered a symbol of resurrection and immortality, the scarab beetle was often depicted in ancient Egyptian art, jewelry, and amulets. It was even common for the deceased to be buried with a scarab amulet to ensure safe passage into the afterlife. The ancient Egyptians believed that the scarab beetle rolling dung balls symbolized the sun's journey across the sky, serving as a metaphor for rebirth and renewal.

In addition to Egypt, beetles were also revered in ancient China. The silkworm beetle, Bombyx mori, played a vital role in the Chinese silk industry. Chinese emperors guarded the secret of silk production for centuries, leading to the formation of the Silk Road and the exchange of goods and knowledge across vast distances. The intricate process of breeding silkworm beetles and harvesting their cocoons became an integral part of Chinese culture and economy. The use of silkworm beetles and the silk they produced symbolized wealth, luxury, and status.

Moving forward in time, beetles continued to leave their mark on human civilization. During the Renaissance, the exploration and discovery of new lands brought about an increased fascination with the natural world. The European voyages of exploration not only led to the discovery of new beetle species but also the introduction of beetles to different parts of the world. As global trade flourished, exotic beetles from far-off lands were collected and showcased in cabinets of curiosity, stimulating scientific curiosity and the study of entomology. These cabinets became instrumental in the development of taxonomy, as scientists sought to understand and categorize the diverse array of beetle species.

The Industrial Revolution marked a turning point in the relationship between humans and beetles. As urbanization and industrialization advanced, beetles faced challenges from pollution, habitat loss, and changes in agricultural practices. The emergence of synthetic dyes also impacted the demand for natural beetle-based dyes, such as cochineal red derived from the scale insect Dactylopius coccus. These changes prompted early discussions on the importance of conserving biodiversity and the need for sustainable practices.

Advancements in scientific understanding during the 20th century revealed the key ecological roles beetles play in ecosystems. Beetles, as decomposers, aid in the breakdown of organic matter, contributing to nutrient cycling and soil health. Some beetles, like dung beetles, help regulate the population of dung-creating animals, enhancing nutrient recycling and reducing disease transmission. These insights into the intricate web of life have influenced conservation efforts and emphasized the significance of protecting beetle populations for the overall health of ecosystems.

In recent years, beetles have found a place in modern technology and medicine. Scientists have begun exploring the potential therapeutic properties of beetle compounds, such as antimicrobial peptides found in certain beetles' exoskeletons. Research into the adaptability and resilience of beetles has also inspired biomimicry, leading to the development of new materials and designs that mimic the beetles' exoskeleton structure and properties. The remarkable capabilities of beetles, such as their ability to withstand extreme temperatures or resist pressure, have sparked innovation in fields ranging from aerospace engineering to architecture.

Furthermore, beetles have left their mark on literature and popular culture. From Franz Kafka's famous novel, "The Metamorphosis," where the protagonist transforms into a giant beetle, to the beloved character of "Herbie" in Disney's "The Love Bug," beetles have captured the imagination of writers, filmmakers, and storytellers. Their diverse forms, colors, and behaviors make them intriguing subjects for creative interpretations, serving as metaphors for transformation, resilience, or even existential questioning.

Beetles have left an indelible mark on human history. They have been revered, studied, and celebrated for their symbolism, economic importance, scientific contributions, and influence on art, design, and literature. From ancient civilizations to the modern era, beetles continue to fascinate and reveal their profound significance in the intricate tapestry of human existence and the natural world. Their presence serves as a reminder of the interconnectedness between humans and the diverse organisms that share our planet, urging us to appreciate, protect, and learn from the wonders of the beetles that surround us.

CHAPTER 10

Beetles in Pop Culture

Throughout history, beetles have captivated and inspired people from all walks of life. These fascinating creatures, with their diverse species and intriguing characteristics, have left a profound mark on our collective imagination. From their inclusion in literature and artwork to their influence on music and fashion, beetles have become an ever-present symbol in popular culture.

A significant example of beetles in pop culture is The Beatles, the legendary English rock band that emerged during the 1960s. Led by John Lennon, Paul McCartney, George Harrison, and Ringo Starr, The Beatles revolutionized the music industry and became cultural icons. Their name itself, with its playful pun on the insect, reflects their whimsical yet innovative approach to music.

The band's exploration of beetles extended beyond their name. Their album covers often featured subtle references to beetles, including their iconic "Abbey Road" album cover. This distinctive image, portraying the band members walking across a zebra crossing with a Volkswagen Beetle parked nearby, has become an enduring symbol of The Beatles' influence and continues to evoke a sense of nostalgia among fans worldwide.

Beetles have also permeated the world of cinema, adding depth to characters and storylines. One such example is the legendary Indiana Jones, portrayed by Harrison Ford in the beloved film series. The character's dedication to archaeological exploration is often associated with his fascination for scarab beetles, which he views as symbols of ancient mysteries waiting to be unraveled. The presence of scarab beetles in the films intensifies the sense of adventure, danger, and intrigue.

In literature, beetles have emerged as powerful symbols, offering thoughtprovoking metaphors for human experiences. Franz Kafka's renowned novella, "The Metamorphosis," explores the existential journey of Gregor Samsa, who inexplicably awakens one morning transformed into a grotesque, insect-like creature. Kafka masterfully employs the symbolism of a beetle to delve into themes of alienation, identity crisis, and the human condition. Through Gregor's transformation, Kafka prompts readers to reflect on their own lives, the pressures of society, and the quest for acceptance.

Beyond their association with music and literature, beetles have influenced various art forms, fashion trends, and advertising campaigns. The striking shapes, colors, and intricate patterns found on beetles have captured the imagination of artists and designers throughout history. Ancient Egyptian scarab amulets have become treasured artifacts, symbolizing rebirth and protection. Contemporary fashion often incorporates beetle motifs, incorporating their allure and mystique into garments and accessories. Furthermore, advertising campaigns have utilized beetles to evoke emotions of elegance, resilience, and adaptability, aligning their brand messaging with the qualities attributed to these remarkable creatures.

Delving deeper into beetles' influence on popular culture, we discover that these creatures have not only influenced the realms of music, literature, art, cinema, and fashion but have also impacted scientific research and environmental conservation efforts. Scientists have long been fascinated by beetles, recognizing their astonishingly diverse adaptations, behaviors, and ecological importance. With over 350,000 known species, beetles make up the largest group of insects on Earth. They inhabit various ecosystems, contributing to pollination, decomposition, and nutrient recycling. This ecological significance has led scientists to study beetles extensively, unlocking insights into their evolutionary history, ecological interactions, and potential applications in fields such as agriculture and medicine.

Furthermore, beetles have become symbols of resilience and adaptability. Their ability to thrive in diverse climates and habitats, ranging from deserts to rainforests, highlights their remarkable capacity to overcome challenges and survive against the odds. This resilience resonates with people facing their own trials and tribulations, offering a source of inspiration and strength.

Intriguingly, beetles have also found their way into various belief systems and cultural practices. In ancient Egypt, scarab beetles held powerful symbolism, representing the sun god Ra's journey across the sky and the concept of rebirth. Scarab amulets were often placed in tombs, believed to offer protection and guide the deceased through the afterlife. In Norse mythology, a giant cosmic beetle named Eikþyrnir inhabited the sacred World Tree, Yggdrasil, symbolizing the interconnectedness of all things. Even today, some cultures revere beetles as symbols of luck, fertility, and transformation.

The enduring presence of beetles in pop culture highlights their timeless appeal and their ability to connect with audiences across generations and continents. They invite us to pause, explore the beauty and diversity of the natural world, and reflect on our place within it. As we immerse ourselves in the world of beetles, we are reminded of the profound impact that even the smallest of creatures can have on our creativity, spirituality, and understanding of the world around us.

CHAPTER 11

Ants in Science Fiction

Beetles have always fascinated humans with their unique appearances, behaviors, and abilities. It is no surprise, then, that these remarkable creatures have found their way into the realms of science fiction literature. In this chapter, we delve into the exploration of beetles in science fiction and explore the various ways they have been depicted in this genre.

Science fiction has long been a platform for authors to push the boundaries of imagination and speculate on what the future might hold. Beetles, with their diverse forms and intriguing behaviors, have provided inspiration for authors to craft fascinating tales. From giant mech beetles used as weapons to intelligent beetlelike alien races, the possibilities are endless.

One popular theme in science fiction is the notion of bioengineering or genetic manipulation, where beetles are often used as a basis for creating fantastical creatures. These genetically modified beetles can possess incredible strength, advanced sensory capabilities, or even the ability to emit harmful toxins. The ethical implications of such bioengineering endeavors are often explored, raising questions about the boundaries we should or shouldn't cross as we tamper with nature. These beetles often serve as formidable adversaries or crucial allies to the protagonists in these stories, highlighting the complex relationships between humans and the creations they engineer.

In other instances, beetles in science fiction take center stage as alien creatures from distant planets. These extraterrestrial beetles come in various shapes, sizes, and colors, transcending the limitations of

Earthbound beetles. Authors often explore the societal structures and advanced technologies of these alien beetle races, offering a unique perspective on intergalactic cultures and civilizations. These stories allow readers to contemplate the vast possibilities of life beyond our own planet and challenge our understanding of what it means to be intelligent or sentient.

Moreover, beetles have been used as inspiration for futuristic technologies and gadgets in science fiction. From robotic beetles that serve as spies or reconnaissance agents to devices that mimic the extraordinary abilities of beetles, such as flight or camouflage, these inventions immerse readers in a world where the boundaries between reality and fiction blur. The exploration of such technology pushes the limits of human ingenuity and invites us to consider the potential applications of biomimicry, where nature becomes the blueprint for innovation.

Science fiction authors also utilize beetles as symbols or metaphors in their stories. These beetles may represent resilience, adaptability, or even the struggle for survival in an ever-changing world. By using beetles in this symbolic manner, authors can explore profound philosophical or moral questions that resonate with readers on a deeper level. They may raise inquiries about human nature, the fragility of life, or the delicate balance of ecosystems, invoking contemplation on our place in the vast tapestry of existence. These stories compel us to reflect on our own actions and their consequences, urging us to consider the impact we have on the world around us.

Moreover, science fiction explores beetles' evolutionary marvels, delving into their intricate anatomical structures and physiological adaptations. Authors, driven by scientific curiosity, delve into the biological mechanisms that enable beetles to survive and thrive in various environments. They investigate the strategies beetles employ to resist extreme temperatures, overcome harsh conditions, or defend against predators. By extrapolating upon these natural abilities, authors stretch the boundaries of plausibility, creating speculative scenarios that challenge our understanding of what is scientifically possible.

Additionally, the cultural significance of beetles is explored in science fiction, drawing inspiration from their importance in different societies throughout history. From the sacred scarab of ancient Egypt, symbolizing rebirth and transformation, to the Japanese myth of the rhinoceros beetle as a symbol of strength and courage, beetles have held various cultural meanings around the world. Science fiction authors tap into these cultural associations, incorporating them into their narratives to enrich the characters and worlds they create. By infusing beetles with cultural significance, authors not only pay homage to the profound impact these creatures have had on human history but also inspire readers to contemplate the symbolism embedded in the natural world.

As we delve into the realm of science fiction, it becomes apparent that beetles offer endless possibilities for storytelling. Their unique characteristics and captivating allure continue to inspire authors to weave tales that captivate readers' imaginations. Whether as tools, adversaries, or symbols, beetles in science fiction bring a touch of wonder and curiosity to the genre, reminding us of the vast potential for innovation and exploration in the world of literature. Through the lens of science fiction, the world of beetles expands beyond our wildest imaginations, inviting us to ponder the marvels of nature, the complexities of ethics, the frontiers of scientific progress, and the multifaceted layers of human culture.

CHAPTER 12

Beetles in Digital Realms

In our modern era of technology and virtual reality, beetles have transcended the physical world and made their way into the digital realm. With the rise of video games, online communities, and virtual pet simulations, beetles have become popular and beloved characters in various digital platforms.

One of the earliest instances of beetles in digital realms can be traced back to the popular Japanese video game series, "Mushiking: The King of Beetles." Released in 2003, this game allowed players to collect, battle, and train virtual beetles in a captivating storyline. The game incorporated elements of strategy, using a RockPaper-Scissors battle mechanic where players had to choose the right attack or defense move based on their beetle's type and attributes. This added depth and complexity to the gameplay, with players developing strategies to create the most effective beetle team. The success of "Mushiking" not only captivated gamers but also inspired toys, merchandise, and even an animated television series, solidifying the influence of beetles in the digital realm.

Following the success of "Mushiking," beetles made appearances in other video game franchises as well. In the beloved "Animal Crossing" series, players come across various beetle species while exploring their virtual village. These beetles, like the Horned Dynastid or the Golden Stag, appear at specific times and locations within the game, adding an element of anticipation and strategy to the gameplay. As players stroll through the lush forests and gardens of their virtual world, they can stumble upon beetles nestled on tree trunks or flying by, creating an immersive and realistic experience.

These beetles can be caught, added to a personal collection, and sometimes even sold for in-game currency, enticing players to dedicate their time to beetle hunting and collection. The inclusion of beetles in "Animal Crossing" serves not only as an entertaining element but also as an educational tool, exposing players to the vast diversity of beetle species and raising awareness about their ecological importance.

Furthermore, beetles have also made their way into the world of online communities and social media. Virtual platforms such as forums, blogs, and social media groups have dedicated spaces for beetle enthusiasts to share their sightings, discuss their behavior, and exchange tips on beetle care and breeding. These platforms have evolved into virtual museums of sorts, where individuals can showcase their beetle collections and engage in spirited debates about rare species, breeding techniques, and proper care. The collective knowledge and experience shared among these enthusiasts not only strengthens their understanding of beetles but also contribute to ongoing scientific research and conservation efforts. As members engage in passionate discussions about proper beetle care, habitat preservation, and even conservation efforts, they continue to deepen their knowledge and understanding of beetles, creating an educational and informative exchange of ideas.

The fascination with beetles in digital realms extends beyond just video games and online communities. Virtual pet simulations, such as "Tamagotchi" and "Nintendogs," have included beetle species as virtual pets for players to care for and interact with. These digital beetles require feeding, cleaning, and attention, simulating the experience of owning and nurturing a real beetle. Players must provide suitable environments, such as terrariums with the right temperature and humidity, and ensure a balanced diet for their virtual beetle pets to thrive. These virtual pets serve as a virtual companion, fostering responsibility, empathy, and a sense of connection with the natural world. As players tend to their virtual beetles, they gain insights into the complexities of beetle care, including feeding habits, environmental needs, and even potential health issues. These simulations not only provide entertainment but also serve as educational tools for individuals interested in owning and caring for real beetles.

The integration of beetles into digital realms serves not only as a means of entertainment and education but also as a way to inspire curiosity and exploration. Virtual beetle encounters allow individuals to learn about different beetle species, their habitats, and their unique characteristics. Whether it be through virtual beetle collections in games like "Mushiking" and "Animal Crossing," engaging discussions in online communities, or virtual pet simulations, the digital representation of beetles sparks interest and encourages further exploration and understanding of the insect world.

As technology continues to advance, we can expect even more innovative ways in which beetles and other insects are incorporated into digital realms. From augmented reality experiences that allow users to interact with virtual beetles in their own surroundings to virtual reality simulations that transport individuals into rich beetle habitats, the possibilities are endless. Imagine putting on a virtual reality headset and finding yourself walking through a lush tropical rainforest, surrounded by the sights and sounds of beetles scuttling through the undergrowth and buzzing overhead. These immersive experiences would allow individuals to observe beetles up close, marvel at their intricate features, and learn about their role in the ecosystem. Such advancements in technology would provide unprecedented opportunities for exploration, education, and connection with the natural world.

Beetles have proven to be versatile and captivating creatures, captivating both the real world and the digital world. Through their presence in video games, online communities, and virtual pet simulations, they have sparked interest, fostered a sense of community, and educated individuals about the diversity and ecological importance of these fascinating insects. As technology continues to evolve, the boundaries between the physical and digital realms blur, offering new and exciting ways to engage with beetles. Whether in pixels or in the wild, the world of beetles will continue to captivate our hearts and minds, reminding us of the wonders that inhabit our planet, both in reality and in the digital expanse.

CHAPTER 13

Fun Facts about Beetles

Beetles are fascinating creatures that have captivated the attention of scientists and nature enthusiasts for centuries. From their incredible diversity to their remarkable adaptations, beetles have plenty of fun facts that will leave you in awe. Let's dive into the fascinating world of beetles and explore some of the most intriguing and entertaining facts about these remarkable insects:

1. Beetle Bonanza:

With over 400,000 known species, beetles make up the largest group of insects on Earth. This astonishing number represents about one-fourth of all known animal species on the planet. Their diversity is mind-boggling, encompassing various ecological niches and habitats. Beetles can be found in almost every corner of the planet, from the Arctic tundra to the Amazon rainforest, from deep sea environments to high mountain ranges. This incredible adaptability has allowed beetles to thrive and occupy diverse ecological roles, making them vital components of ecosystems worldwide.

2. Master Architects:

Some beetles, like the leaf-rolling weevils, are skilled architects in their own right. These crafty insects exhibit an exceptional ability to manipulate leaves, rolling them into tubes varying in complexity. They use their mandibles to cut leaf fragments and then carefully tuck them into secure positions, creating a protective and cozy environment for their eggs and young ones. Leaf-rolling beetles have perfected the art of leaf manipulation over millions of years, ensuring their survival and the survival of their offspring in a world full of dangers.

3. Glow in the Dark:

Few beetles possess the ability to bioluminesce or "glow in the dark." Fireflies, also known as lightning bugs, are perhaps the most well-known examples of bioluminescent beetles. Both males and females produce light utilizing a complex chemical reaction. Fireflies use specialized light organs, located on their lower abdomen, to create and control their mesmerizing glow. These enchanting creatures synchronize their flashing patterns, creating beautiful displays that light up summer nights in many parts of the world. Fireflies use their captivating light to communicate with potential mates, signaling their availability and compatibility through specific flash patterns and timing.

4. Elusive Jewel:

The scarab beetle, famously associated with ancient Egyptian culture, was considered sacred and symbolized rebirth and regeneration. These beetles were believed to possess divine qualities, thanks to their ability to roll balls of dung and bury them as a source of food. The ancient Egyptians observed the scarab's behavior and noticed that they would lay their eggs within these dung balls, allowing their young to hatch and emerge. This cycle of emerging from decay became a powerful metaphor for resurrection and rebirth in ancient Egyptian religious beliefs. The shiny metallic exoskeletons of scarab beetles were believed to resemble precious gemstones and were often used in jewelry and art to honor their significance.

5. Impressive Strength:

Don't be fooled by their small size – beetles are incredibly strong! The horned beetles, such as the rhinoceros beetle, possess remarkable strength, capable of carrying objects up to 850 times their own body weight. This strength is not only due to their size but also their uniquely structured exoskeletons that act as supportive armor. The elytra, the hardened forewings of beetles, provide a sturdy shield, allowing them to carry heavy loads without compromising their mobility. In addition to their impressive might, male rhinoceros beetles also use their distinct horns to engage in battles for mates and territory, showcasing their strength and dominance. These battles can be intense and determined, with the strongest beetle claiming the right to reproduce and pass on their genes.

6. Gourmet Diners:

Some beetles have unique diets that may surprise you. The long-horned beetle larvae, for instance, feed on decaying wood, playing a crucial role in forest ecosystems by breaking down dead trees and recycling nutrients back into the soil. These wood-boring beetles possess specialized enzymes that allow them to digest and extract nutrients from the tough plant fibers, contributing to the decomposition process. They contribute to the nutrient cycling and regeneration of forest ecosystems. Dung beetles, as their name suggests, feast on animal waste, playing an essential role in maintaining the balance of ecosystems by reducing the presence of animal droppings. By burying and consuming dung, they not only recycle nutrients but also control the population of parasites and pests associated with waste. Dung beetles are ecosystem engineers, shaping the landscape and positively influencing the health of their habitats.

7. Camouflage Experts:

Many beetles are masters of disguise, blending seamlessly into their surroundings to evade predators or catch their prey. The peppered moth beetle, for example, can adapt the color and pattern of its exoskeleton to match its habitat, making it almost invisible to predators. This incredible adaptive ability, known as cryptic coloration, allows them to survive and thrive in their respective environments. They rely on their chitinous exoskeleton and specialized color cells called chromatophores to change their appearance. Similarly, bark beetles boast unique patterns and textures on their exoskeletons, enabling them to blend with the bark of trees effortlessly. Their camouflage helps protect them from potential predators while they go about their vital work of breaking down and recycling dead wood. This is particularly important for forests, as bark beetles, in their natural densities, contribute to the health and regeneration of the ecosystem by thinning out weaker trees, promoting space for new growth.

8. Beetle Music:

Some beetles produce sounds as a means of communication. The stag beetles, with their distinctive antler-like mandibles, engage in fierce battles for territory and mates. These interactions are accompanied by loud hissing or squeaking sounds, creating an eerie symphony in the night. The sounds serve as warnings to rival males and attract attention from potential mates. The males use their mandibles not only as formidable weapons in these battles but also as resonating chambers to amplify their calls. Stag beetle fights are dramatic displays of strength and determination, as the males lock mandibles and push against each other amidst the reverberating sound, showcasing their strength and dominance to secure mating rights.

These are just a few of the numerous fun facts about beetles. From their incredible diversity and adaptations to their roles in ecosystems and remarkable behaviors, beetles continue to surprise and captivate us. Next time you spot a beetle, take a moment to appreciate its remarkable attributes and the vital roles that these diverse insects play in the intricate tapestry of our natural world.

GLOSSARY

Glossary

Antennae:

These are like a beetle's built-in nose and ears. They use these long, thin feelers on their heads to smell, feel, and even taste things around them.

Beetles (Coleoptera):

Beetles are a huge group of insects with tough backs and wings. There are more kinds of beetles than any other type of animal on Earth

Biodiversity:

This is a fancy word for all the different kinds of living things in a place. Beetles add a lot to biodiversity because there are so many types of them.

Bioluminescent Beetles:

These beetles are like natural night lights. They can glow in the dark, just like fireflies!

Bombardier Beetle:

A cool beetle that can shoot a hot, stinky spray from its rear end when it feels threatened. It's like their superpower for protection!

Carnivorous Beetles:

These are beetles that eat other animals. They're like the lions of the beetle world, helping to keep other insect populations under control.

Clown Beetle:

A beetle known for its bright colors and funny behavior. They're the jokers of the beetle family.

Decomposition:

This is when dead plants and animals get broken down into simpler stuff. Beetles help a lot with this, making sure that nutrients return to the earth.

Diurnal and Nocturnal Behavior:

Some beetles are active during the day (diurnal), and others prefer the night (nocturnal). Just like some people are morning persons and others are night owls!

Dung Beetle:

These beetles love poop! They roll it into balls and use it for food and to lay their eggs. It might sound gross, but they're super important for keeping places clean and healthy.

Ecosystem Indicators:

Beetles can tell us a lot about how healthy an environment is. If certain beetles are missing from a place, it might mean something is wrong there.

Elytra:

The hard wing covers on a beetle's back. They're like a built-in shield to protect their delicate wings underneath.

Entomology:

This is the study of insects. People who study beetles and other bugs are called entomologists.

Exoskeleton:

Beetles have a hard outer shell, kind of like wearing armor all the time. It helps them stay safe from harm.

Forests, Grasslands, Wetlands:

These are different homes for beetles. Forests have lots of trees, grasslands are like big open fields, and wetlands are wet, swampy areas. Beetles live in all these places and more!

Gourmet Diners:

Some beetles have very special diets. For example, long-horned beetle babies eat wood, and some beetles even like to dine on fungi!

Habitat Diversity:

Beetles live in all sorts of places, from forests to deserts to even under the water. They're really good at making homes in many different environments

Hercules Beetles:

Big, strong beetles with horns on their heads. They're like the superheroes of the beetle world because of their strength.

Invasive Beetle Species:

These are beetles that have moved into places where they don't naturally belong. They can sometimes cause problems for the plants and animals that live there.

Larva:

This is what a baby beetle looks like. It's kind of like a caterpillar and eventually turns into a grown-up beetle.

Master Architects:

Some beetles are amazing at building things. Like the leaf-rolling weevils that can turn leaves into safe little homes for their babies.

Metamorphosis:

This is a fancy way of saying "change." Beetles go through a big change as they grow up, turning from larvae to pupae to adult beetles.

Molting:

When a beetle grows, it sheds its old skin and grows a new one. It's like getting a new set of clothes that fit better!

Pupa:

A stage in a beetle's life when it's changing from a larva into an adult. It's like they're in a cozy sleeping bag, getting ready to wake up as a grown-up beetle.

Taxonomy:

This is how scientists organize and classify living things, like putting them into groups. Beetles have their own group because they have similar features.

ABOUT US

About Us

The Bug Collective, founded by a dad and his two sons, is an inspiring family venture rooted in a shared passion for the fascinating world of insects.

Born from a simple backyard exploration, their interest in bugs blossomed into a creative endeavor. They aim to craft engaging and informative books about the entomological wonders they discover.

Through their work, they seek to ignite curiosity and foster a deeper appreciation for the intricate lives of bugs in readers young and old. The Bug Collective is more than a publishing venture; it's a celebration of nature's tiny marvels, brought to you by a family that finds joy in every creepy crawler and fluttering wing.

www.ingramcontent.com/pod-product-compliance
Lightning Source LLC
Chambersburg PA
CBHW080744120726
48001CB00009B/2672